MW01537669

unboxed memories

poetry and prose

adela muhić

for anyone that needs it

i hope you find someone that wants to write about you because you'd be an interesting story to tell
-it ain't me

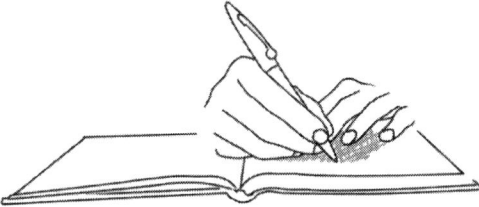

adela muhic

2

i've unlocked the memories
and thrown away the key
they're here now
for you and for me

adela muhic

i have to tell you
it didn't feel right when he held me
laying in his bed instead of yours
only made me feel even more alone
i don't fit him the way i fit you and
i didn't feel anything in my heart
i had suddenly gone numb and i didn't want anything
except to be back into your arms
what'd you do to me?

adela muhic

october

i will never understand how somebody that wasn't
meant for me, could understand me so well
i will never understand how something
that was so wrong, felt so right
i will never understand how a cold night in october
with him felt like a warm night in july
i will never understand
but, maybe it's better if i don't

i hate those two minutes i have in between tasks
because in that two minute gap is when you cross my
mind and you don't leave
everything replays in those two minutes
trying to pinpoint the exact moment we lost it
and in those two minutes i wish for nothing else
except for you to be by my side
& then it's over

adela muhic

you know what hurts?
the fact that you read my
most vulnerable words
and replied
"i'd pick you"
and then you didn't

adela muhic

i didn't care that you thought about her
while you were with me
i just cared that you were with me
you called me by her name last night

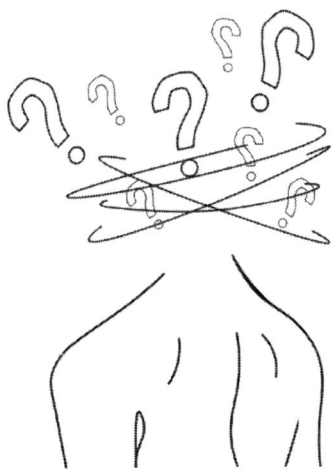

adela muhic

you knew exactly how to look at me
and where to touch me
and what words to whisper against my skin
to get me back to you
and it worked.
every. fucking. time.
i still don't forgive myself

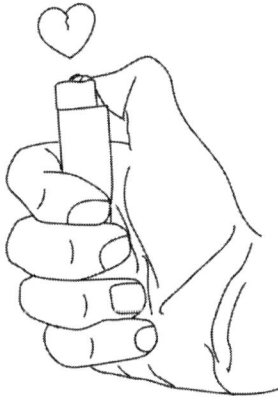

adela muhic

should that mean something?
that when i'm drunk off of this vodka
that you're the only one i'm thinking of
and the only one i want to talk to
i want to hear your voice right now so bad
it's 1am and i just want to hear you tell me it's okay
and that you want to be with me
even though deep down we both know it's not true
tell me lies
it's what i need to hear
right now
from you
please

it was poetry
the way you looked at me in the morning
the way your hands roamed my body in the night
the way our souls intertwined themselves
almost as seamlessly as our fingers did
it was pure poetry
and then you told me you hated poetry

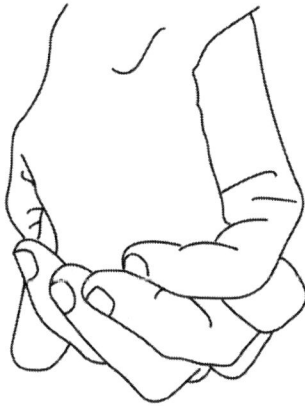

adela muhic

you tried to get me to fight for you
but i can't
you were never really mine to begin with

you will always be my favorite "maybe"

i'm sorry
i'm not used to somebody wanting to stay
and i don't know how to write about you
when all i've known
is emptiness in relationships
and all you've taught me
is what a relationship should be
so, i'm sorry,
i'm not used to somebody wanting to stay

don't use me to fill your void

the kisses between the laughs

i painted a perfect picture of us two
do you want to know what it looked like?
it was our favorite scene
the one where we're walking
with our fingers intertwined
and i keep trying to match your pace
and then you intentionally bump into
me and i lose my balance
we're throwing each other off
and can't stop laughing about it
i tug your hand to pull you down to me
just so i can give you
a few kisses between the laughs
yeah... that's the perfect picture.
the kisses between the laughs.
i think that's what i'll call it.

adela muhic

i wish you had told me
you had no intention of keeping me

adela muhic

32

when i'm laying under my blankets and comforted by
the soft droplets of the rain pattering against my
window, that's when i think of you
and what you're going to be like
will you enjoy the rain like i do?
are you the type to toss and turn in your sleep?
how much of the cover will you steal from me
when i'm not looking?
i just hope you enjoy the rain as much as i do
because none of the ones before you seemed to
sometimes i'm the rain

adela muhic

i hate staying up past midnight
because the hours between 1am to 4am
are reserved for you and only you
i keep busy to not think of you
it's not working

adela muhic

it's 2:35 am and the rain won't stop
it's pouring onto my window & not letting me sleep
i hate it when this happens
it's as if i'm being taunted by the loud winds
they're repeating your name as a reminder that
you don't lay with me anymore

i'm going to go to sleep
and i'm going to try not to dream of you
except it's so hard
when i see us so happy together
you're saying all the right things
and i'm falling in love so fast
almost as fast as the time we had to run in
because it was raining so hard outside
but you wanted to show me how bright
the stars were shining for me
it's as if they put on a show for us,
they knew we were watching them
all we did was laugh when we got
into the house about how soaked
our clothes were
you wrapped your fingers around mine
and i was finally at peace
i wish it wasn't only in my dreams

you told me you loved me
and i couldn't do anything else but kiss you
because i didn't have the words to tell you
i don't feel the same way anymore
i'm sorry

adela muhic

i haven't found you yet, but when i do,
i'm just going to give you these words
and hope it's enough

sincerely,
yours

adela muhic

maybe the reason i keep pushing you away
is because i don't believe i'm worth the stay

adela muhic

i've been feeling so uninspired lately
and i have no idea what to do about it
where should i go?
who should i talk to?
is there a hand i should be holding?
or arms that should be holding me?
when will i find my answer?

to be so lonely

because that's what happens when you get lonely and confide in anybody. you settle for the first person that gives you any amount of attention. you think it's worth it in the moment, you just want to hold onto the feeling for a little while longer. it doesn't last because it was a temporary feeling, but you already knew that. you knew what you were doing and yet you did it anyways. you did it to yourself. don't do it anymore. it's better to be lonely than to be surrounded by temporary people.

why did you want me to be the one that got away?
why did you never ask me to stay?

adela muhic

52

adela muhic

i can tell you're coming from
a place of hurt when you hurt me
i don't know who she is that hurt you
but i'm not her
all i wanted to do was wrap my arms around your
insecurities and give you reassurance
i wanted to save you
but i know i'd only lose myself in the process of that

adela muhic

okok

okok

i hope you don't think twice about letting me go
i hope you don't ever get the urge
to call and apologize to me
i hope you don't repeat our last conversation
i hope you move on with somebody that you think
you're a perfect fit for
and i hope you don't think twice about letting me go
because i won't come back

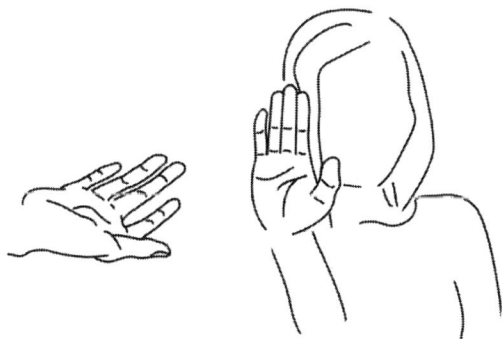

adela muhic

i didn't need you to come back
and confuse me like that
but you did, because that's what you always do
and i fell for it, because that's what i always do

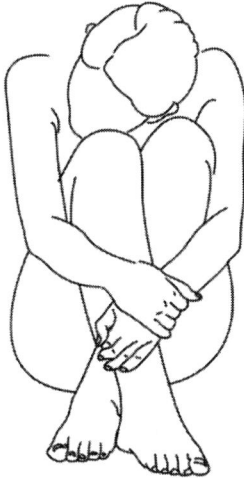

adela muhic

i almost loved you and we almost made it

i just don't understand
how you lied so easily
how every feeling was fake
and every kiss was out of lust
why did you disguise yourself
in order to get what you wanted?
that's so fucking evil.
and despite it all,
i would never even think of doing that to you.

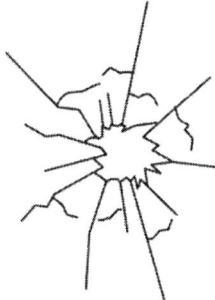

adela muhic

maybe after a couple of bottles,
i won't think about you anymore.
-the lies i keep telling myself-

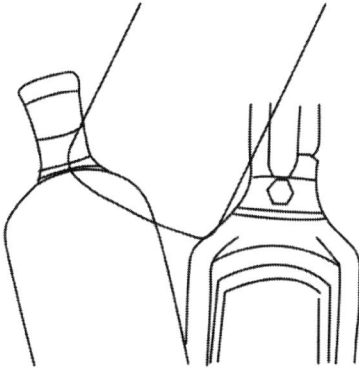

adela muhic

it's been a month
since we fell apart
since you cared
since you held my hand
since you called me *yours*
it's been a month
since we fell apart
but the truth is,
we fell apart a long time ago
we just didn't know how to let go
i still don't know

adela muhic

<u>i know you</u>
you don't want closure, you just want to see if
he's going to try to fight for you again
you're not going to say your final goodbye
and you're not going to tell him to leave you be
you're going to let him manipulate you into
giving him another chance that he doesn't deserve
i know you, because i used to be you

<u>i'm hurt for the girl i was when he broke me</u>
she had high hopes yet she settled for less than she
should've. she started to contradict herself. i watched
as she tried to hold him to a high standard only to
end up accepting the lowest version he presented.
she knew what she deserved even though she was
happy with the tiny pieces he gave. it was okay for a
while until she was finally broken down to her core.
she was stripped down to the last of herself and was
left with no option but to rebuild herself. but, that's a
good thing. because when she finally came back, she
didn't need validation from you or from him. she was
in a place where no single person's opinion could
affect what she knows to be true. she doesn't even
realize that i'm writing this for her as she lays in my
bed with her legs crossed. i'm unsure of where i'm
headed with these words but all i know is i want her
to love them as much as i love her.
you know her name.

i don't think that's what love is
i don't think that you're supposed
to spend all of your time fixing someone
no matter how much you want to help them
everyone has to battle their demons by themselves

i'm laying here and i'm thinking about
the endless conversations i'd like to have with you
but i'm not picking up my phone to call you
and it just kinda hit me
i wonder how much we've missed out on
just because we held ourselves back out of fear
fear of what the other person would say
fear of being rejected by someone you want
fear of thinking we're not good enough

adela muhic

one of the hardest things you'll have to do
is accept the fact that you're not right for someone
no matter how badly you want to be
the quicker you accept that fact,
the easier it'll be to get over them
at least that's what i keep telling myself

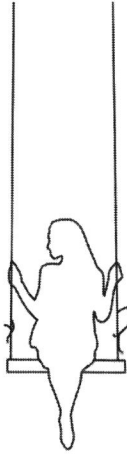

adela muhic

i searched for parts of you in him, but
he doesn't hold my hand the way you did
and his lips don't sync with mine the way yours did
his body doesn't understand mine and
his laugh doesn't make me laugh the way yours did
but, most importantly,
his heart is not made for me the way yours was

adela muhic

everything i had in me,
i handed over to the wrong person
so when it came to you and you asked me
if i was ready to give my all to you
all i could do was break down and cry
because i didn't even have all of me anymore

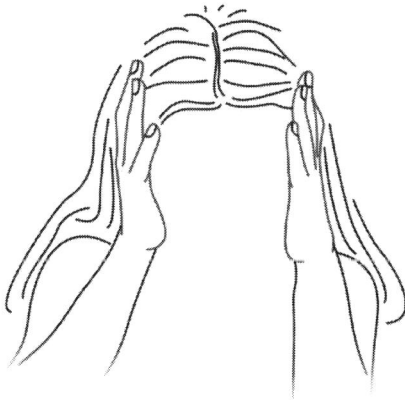

adela muhic

and as much as you hurt me,
i have to recognize that i hurt you right back
maybe even twice as hard
for that i'm sorry, i'm so sorry
i never would've wanted you to feel
the hurt and pain that you once caused me

adela muhic

i am at peace
knowing that although i am no longer
receiving your love, it is going to somebody
that needed to be healed more than i did
it's okay, i promise

i think i had to do that
i had to get lost in a person
i had to let myself completely drown in a toxic love
in order to learn what's wrong in love & what's right
i had to lose myself in you and then lose you
to find myself again. and i'm okay with that.
i'll always choose myself. everytime.

adela muhic

the issues you had with her
became the issues you had with me
i'm sorry she broke your trust and
i'm sorry i couldn't repair it
but that's not my job

i thought if i gave you all of me,
it'd make you stay
never did i think it'd be the thing
that would drive you away

i construct the best art
after you leave me in pieces

adela muhic

"i don't open up to anybody"

"doesn't it get lonely, then?"

i miss you so much
why did you change your mind about me?
what did i do to make you change your mind?
why didn't you want me the way i wanted you?
it's 4am and i can't sleep

how ironic is it that i can't stop cursing your name by
day yet i fall asleep in your shirt every night?
i hate what you've done to me

adela muhic

i hope we never meet again
i hope your tongue forgets my name
i hope your hands forget my curves
i hope your ears forget my voice
i hope your heart forgets my love
and i hope you finally forget about me

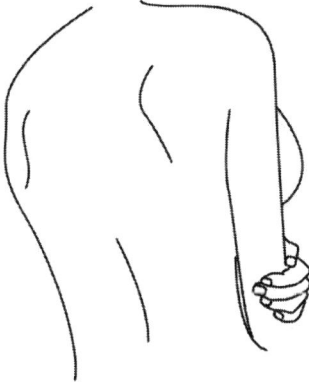

adela muhic

i'm at a really strange point in my life
i now understand that i'm worthy of love
but i wouldn't know what to do with it
even if it showed up on my front doorstep

i wrote out my love for you on paper
and i handed it over to you
you handed it back and told me
you didn't understand
then i spent the whole night rewriting it
to better accommodate your tastes
until the morning came and i realized
i can't make you understand my love
if it's not meant for you

and when she finally walked away,
it was with her head held high
and dignity on display
it takes time, but you'll get there

her fire drew me to her
i should've known i'd get burned
but it was worth it
if i could only hold her hand one more time
and let her know that she's awakened
something in me that i forgot i had

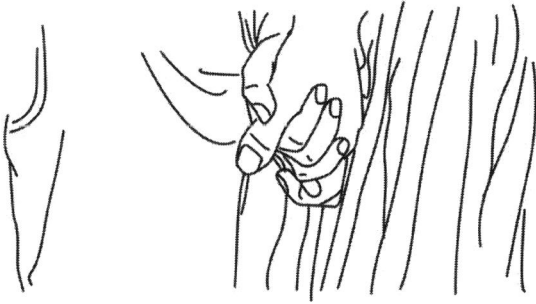

adela muhic

i fell in love with you so easily at 2am
the moonlight illuminated the path we took
and the wind pushed us towards each other
we were laughing at anything and everything
in the midst of it i realized
i don't ever want to lose this moment
i don't ever want to lose you
all you have to do is stay

adela muhic

110

it's never too late to fall in love with yourself

people will always make mistakes, that's inevitable
second chances are something we all yearn for
i guess the question i keep repeating is:
why wasn't i worth getting it right on the first try?

even at your worst, i still thought you were the best
my mistake

i'm not who i used to be
and i never plan on going back to her

adela muhic

i'd rather lose you a million times over
before i ever lose myself again
i was blind when it came to you

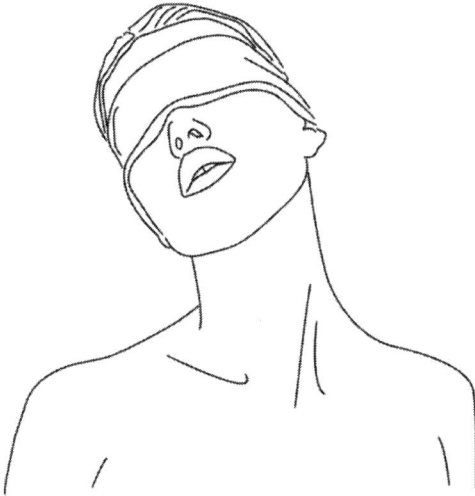

i'll forgive every single thing you did to me,
but if i forget about it then i put myself at risk
of experiencing it again
i don't think i'd survive you a second time

i held your hand in attempt of saving you from the
insecurities you were drowning in
but all you did was drag me down with you
when it was my turn to drown,
you didn't even notice
why do you keep doing this to me?

you were just a risk i couldn't take
maybe if you understood how long it took me
to climb this mountain of darkness
you'd understand why
i stay as far away from the edge as possible
you were pushing me to the edge

we can race through the sunflower field all day
until our feet grow tired if you'd like
or we could ride the waves in the evening
as the sun sets if you'd prefer that
i'll travel coast to coast, anywhere you want,
as long as i'm with you

the days are getting longer and longer
now that you're gone
the sun doesn't even want to shine on me anymore
it's as if she's mad at me for letting you walk away
i want her to know that i'm mad at myself, too
i wonder if it's like that for you, wherever you are
maybe we'll meet again one day
when we're both better

adela muhic

how close do you think we were to getting it right?
i need to quit asking myself that question
i'm dying to get an answer
but the sky is tired of hearing me repeat myself

adela muhic

at one point being in his arms felt like
i was finally home
and now i can't picture a worse place to be

at the end of the night,
when the music stops and the lights turn on
and everyone ends up leaving with someone else
i'll still be here for you
even though you don't deserve it
i was always there for you when nobody else was

the love that you keep searching for
is hidden inside of you
i can't be the one to find it for you
but i hope you figure it out soon

you told me you wouldn't be good for me
how foolish of me to think you'd at least
try to better yourself for me
that was my first mistake, loving you was my second

adela muhic

it's hard holding on to somebody
that let go of you a long time ago

adela muhic

i could smell the whiskey on your breath
as you tried to convince me to stay the night
the broken glass on the ground told me
it was time for me to go
i know it's killing you realizing that you've hurt the
only person that would never hurt you

adela muhic

why are you killing yourself for someone
that hasn't even noticed your absence?

adela muhic

i fell in love with your drunken words
but you didn't know how to love me sober

you're gonna go out and drink your worries away
and you'll take home the first girl you see
it won't be long until you realize she's not me
she might order the same drink i did or even wrap
her arms around your body like i used to
but she won't know where to kiss you on your neck
and she won't know how to hold you when it's over
when she leaves in the morning,
you'll realize i was the only one willing to stay
i'm not the kind of girl you can get over in one night

adela muhic

you turned into the same person you warned me about

when your fingers trailed their way down my spine
i could feel the coldness radiating from you
from where the love once used to be
it was over. it was well over at that point.
the moment i knew you had fallen out of love

adela muhic

we'll meet again, but as strangers
we won't have the same smiles anymore
& we won't embrace each other as before
but, the love? the love will always be there
just not like it once was

adela muhic

156

even the city lights can't shine as bright as you do

if i can write this many pages about the wrong ones,
imagine the books i'll write about the right one

we slipped away into the night
where we danced until our feet were sore
and laughed until our stomachs hurt
a part of me knew it wouldn't last long
we lost the love as quick as we found it

adela muhic

i now have scars where your love once used to be

i know our story is coming to an end
i keep trying to rewrite the ending
but i'm running out of pages and
this pen is almost out of ink and
i can't think of what i want my
last words to you to be

adela muhic

you said you'd come home to me,
when the summer came to an end.
the leaves started changing their colors,
and you changed yours too.
and i was the last one to find out.

adela muhic

i feel like i knew you before we even met -
maybe somewhere in a different lifetime
our paths crossed and we promised to
always find our way back to one another
and, here we are, ready to love each other again

i wasn't ready to become
just another memory of yours

i hope one day
you love yourself
as much as i love you

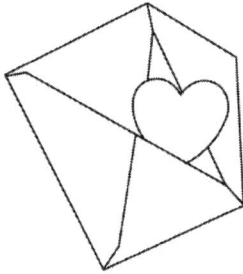

you stopped calling me baby and
it's clear what you've been doing lately
the messages stopped coming and
we saw each other less and less
you turned me into such a mess
i just hope she never does to you
what you did to me

i screamed at the top of my lungs
and yet somehow you still overlooked my pain

adela muhic

178

<u>brutally honest</u>

he said to me, "you keep writing about love because even though you don't have it, that's all you want. you're just scared of it now" and i hated how right he was. we didn't talk anymore after that. why can't i let anyone in? was all of that true? am i just craving the things i can't have? do i even want it again? i barely made it out last time, how many more times do i have to try before i get it right?

the right person will turn anybody into a poet

Hi.

Thank you so much for taking the time out of your day to read my book and live out these stories with me. I hope you were able to find parts of yourself in this and it helped you in some way. If there's anything you take away from this, I hope it's the fact that you realize you are not alone and that we all experience many of the same things just in different ways.
It always gets better.

-

To the writer that hasn't realized their potential yet, the world is ready for your story whenever you're ready to tell it. Don't be afraid to take that risk, it's worth it. I promise.

-

To my family and friends, thank you for supporting me through this book and all of my other crazy ideas. I love you guys more than anything and I couldn't do it without you.
Alhamdulillah for everything.

Adela Muhic

Made in the USA
Las Vegas, NV
10 January 2022

41024824R00103